Table of Contents

Introductions
Chapter 1- Mind Over Matte.
Chapter 2- From Childhood to Adu.
Chapter 3- Face Your Fears
Chapter 4- Keep Strong
Chapter 5- Passions
Chapter 6- Desire
Chapter 7- Determination
Chapter 8- Who is in your Inner Circles
Chapter 9- Overcoming Obstacles
Chapter 10- Wisdom vs. Knowledge
Chapter 11- The Life Map
Chapter 12- The Inner Map
Chapter 13- 90% vs. 10%
Chapter 14- The 9 Principles of Life
Chapter 15- The Comfort Zone
Chapter 16- The Mental Shift
Chapter 17- Understand Your Personality Colors

Introduction
About Me

The Mindset of An Underdog

I was born on October 14, 1982 at 3:46 a.m. at Methodist Hospital in Gary, Indiana to Jan E. Williams (Wilson) and LeRoy D. Moore Jr. My mother always told me, since I learned to talk and walk, I was a goofball. As I grew up, I was always labeled as goofy. When I was young, I was diagnosed with Borderline Intellectual Functioning Disability (BIFD). I went to Tradewinds, which is a special school where children with special needs and disabilities can receive help. Growing up was always hard and sometimes I always wondered "Why am I here?"

I had a tough time in my childhood, as far as school and life. I had a difficult time comprehending faster than normal kids. I felt like I was different, so I tried to the center of attention, or in other words, I became the class clown. Some of my family members thought I would always be a class clown and goofy. I had friends, but I hid all my pain from everyone, including my family. I used to be in my own world, which people used to think I was weird for doing that.

When I was eight, I started learning impersonation, so I could learn how to impersonate others and myself. I always wanted to be an actor, but everyone I knew told me I would never be able to do it. All I would get was criticism. They always criticized the way I walked, talked, sang, and danced. A lot of people thought I was weird because I would walk down the street singing and dancing, even the way I dressed would cause people to judge me. I used to get bullied in elementary school. I would later learn martial arts to defend myself.

A lot of people always told me that I would never amount to anything. It was the constant judgment and criticism that I received growing up that caused me to learn different things to prove them wrong. While people talked about me behind my back, they didn't understand my life. I wanted to be different from everyone else. I wanted to live life how I chose. I guess that made me weird to a lot of people. You see despite others' perspectives, I always knew that I was sent here to change the world and make an impact in the lives of others.

In 2004, I thought I had met my soul mate. In 2006, we had our baby girl named Carmen. In 2007, we had our baby boy named KeJuan Jr.. In 2009, we had another baby boy named Jayden. In 2010, we had our second baby girl named Keyona. In 2012, we had our third baby boy named Imanuel. We had five children together, as well as I helped raise her three sons (Dominico, Dario, and Damerio). They are my sons no matter what and I treat them as such.

In 2013, the worst day of my life happened. This was the day my eight children were taken away from us. I felt like a failed as a father. I became suicidal and I found myself at the Pedestrian Bridge at 3 a.m. getting ready to jump. I yelled to god "Is this what you want me to do? If not then send me a sign!" I received a phone call from a good friend asking me what I had been up to because he told me he had a feeling something was wrong in his spirit about me. He said, "Where are you at?" I responded ". . . the Pedestrian Bridge." He told me to stay where I was at and that he was on his way to come get me. When we got back to his house, he told me to get some rest, get my mind right, and that we would talk the next morning. When morning came, Manifest told me I could stay there until I got back on my feet. Also, he wrote something down on a piece of paper that will always stick with me. He told me not to open the folded paper until he told me to. Three days later he asked me how I was feeling. I told him my mind was clearer and I was ready to start the fight for my children. Manifest told me "Read the paper now." I went to go get the paper and opened it in front of him. It stated, "I will tear down your house and in three days I will rebuild it." Manifest had started working with me on personal development and strengthening my relationship with God.

These were my obstacles and struggles. Now, you will find out exactly how I overcame each hardship and what happens to the struggles I faced as you continue to read through my book.

Chapter 1
Mind Over Matter

- *Self-awareness*
- *Self-talk*
- *Mirror Battle*
- *What are you listening to?*
- *Who are you listening to?*
- *Thought process*
- *Think clearly*
- *Stop stressing*
- *Observation*
- *What is your mentality?*
- *Negative vs. positive*
- *Open your mind*
- *Vivid vision*
- *Light a Fire*
- *What is your 'Why'?*

Self-Awareness
- You have to be aware at all times.
- What do you have to be aware of?

- **Some people will be against you, such as friends, family, loved ones, significant others, and even random people.**

  Your friends will be there for you in your face, but as soon as you're not around some may talk about you behind your back because they haven't been given the vision that you have. They don't want to see you succeed because they're afraid you may leave them behind. This is exactly like the *crab in the barrel,* where one crab is trying to get out of the crate, but the rest of the crabs are trying to pull the single crab back down to the bottom. Sometimes your own family may even be against you because no one can see your vision but you. Even if you try to explain it, they will be unable to comprehend and/or understand your vision because it is not meant for anyone but yourself.

  When you try to show them by example, family may find every reason for you not to complete your vision. In my case, family members would tell me, "I'm just looking out for you", "That's a crazy idea", or "They're just trying to take advantage of you!" I will tell you this one thing from experience- always believe that you can achieve anything you envision.

  For instance, I told my cousin that I wanted to be a motivational speaker. Do you want to take a guess what he told me? He told me that I wouldn't be able to achieve my vision because I'm "too goofy." I was even told, "What are you going to talk about? Video, games and being a superhero." Even though he is my cousin and I love him, but for him to say those statements to me, it felt like he was trying to crush my dreams and that hurt a lot. Despite his comments, I still continued to pursue making my dream of becoming a motivational speaker into a reality. Family is supposed to be there for you, not criticize and cast stones at you, unlike my cousin. Also, family is supposed to serve as a support system to your goals, not bash your dreams/vision.

Now, the biggest negative barrier you will need to be aware of is a relationship, which does not provide support and encouragement, such as a boyfriend, girlfriend, wife, and/or husband. You may be closer to this person than you are to your own family. You may be connected to this person on a deeper level physically, emotionally, and mentally. The relationship may be the most intimate relationship you may have experienced. Your significant other is supposed to be your partner and backbone. You can get a vision and share it with your significant other; however, he or she may find something negative about it. For example, my kids' mother always criticized me when I would share with her my vision and began to work toward fulfilling my vision. She always compared everything to my last vision that didn't turnout as planned. Whenever, I tried to do something positive, she would tell me that I was either "dumb" or "stupid" for doing whatever it was I was doing at the time. A girlfriend, boyfriend, wife, or husband is supposed to build your dream up, not tear it down.

So I'll tell you a piece of advice. Always tell your significant other up front that you have dreams you plan to accomplish. You will not want to be in a relationship with someone that will bash and dump on your dreams. Also, find out if he or she has dreams as well. Together, uplift and encourage one another to accomplish the vision.

The last type you will have to be aware of is random people. They will come out when you least expect it. Some people will tell you that they have seen you before, but you still aren't successful yet. These interactions can cause self-doubt and impact your ability to successfully move forward to accomplish your vision. You see what they fail to understand is real success doesn't come fast and in a hurry, but it takes focus and hard work. For example, this guy I used to know saw me walking one day and he knew that I had started my own business. He said to me "You're still doing that coffee thing and you don't have a car yet?" Then he continued to say, "They're just taking advantage of you." Instead of responding with words, I decided to walk away from him with the reasoning I wasn't going to allow his negative comments and judgment to be a cancer to me. My *'why'* is way too strong.

So please be aware of your surroundings and who you choose to listen to.

Self-Talk
- You have to motivate yourself.
- How do you motivate yourself?
- **Make a video of yourself saying something positive and look at it daily.**
  Record yourself doing a speech or short conversations to yourself. While preparing for the video, think like that video is your future self. You can look at the video each day as a daily reminder of your purpose. This video just might be exactly what you need to get motivated and stay motivated.
- **Write affirmations and read daily.**
  You may have to write down multiple affirmations aligning with your purpose. Affirmations should be specific, direct, and bold statements used to encourage yourself and/or state what you want in life.
- **You can always pray too.**

A prayer can always help too. When you have doubts always pray. Pray for strength to overcome any and every obstacle.

Mirror Battle
- You have to argue with yourself sometimes.
- How do you argue with yourself?
- **Look at yourself in the mirror and yell at yourself whenever you feel like you are about to quit.**
  Sometimes you have to yell at yourself. Don't worry about people looking and hearing you. Not everyone is meant to understand the process. No one else will understand that your biggest enemy is your inner self.
- **Yell at yourself when you are about to lose focus on your goals.**
  When you are about to lose focus, tell yourself not to lose focus. Never lose focus on your dreams, goals, and vision God has given to you.
- **Talk down to the negative side and uplift the positive side.**
  When you see something negative or when someone talks negatively to you, then you may start thinking negative about yourself and your vision. You may have to yell at the negative side of yourself in order for your positive side to shine. The positive will outshine the negative. Your positive is more powerful than you could ever imagine.

What are you Listening to?
- You need to listen to certain things.
- What do you listen to?
- **Always pick a mentor and listen to what he/she says.**
  Find someone who is wiser than you. Find someone who is doing or has done what it is you are trying to do in life. Learn from him/her and do what he/she are doing and has done.
- **Listen to a motivational audio.**
  Buy motivational CDs to listen and reflect. I encourage you to listen to speakers, such as Jim Rohn, Les Brown, Tony Robbins, and Napoleon Hill. These are just to name a few. When you listen take notes and listen multiple times.
- **Listen to inspiration videos.**
  When you start to have self-doubt and fear, listen to different inspirational speakers. You can use specific quotes from speakers as encouragement and motivation.

You may even see a quote somewhere else. Write it down and look at your quotes repeatedly so you do not lose focus.

Who are you listening to?
- Be careful to who you are listening and talking to.
- Why is it importance to have discernment?
- **Some people will always talk down to you about what is it you are trying to accomplish.**
  People are born too quick to judge, sometimes it's in the environment he/she has grown around. They always don't think before speaking or may even think they are helping you, but in actuality their words are hurting you.

- **Some people may deter you from your vision.**
  Certain people are like crabs in a barrel. They see you trying to get free from the barrel, but because of their negativity attempt to pull you back down into the barrel. That's just like life. People may see you try to do something that can change your life and attempt to prevent it. They are so wrapped up in so much negativity that they will criticize you and try to break down your vision because they simply do not have your vision. They just want to complain about life and not change their circumstances. If they see you doing well, it may start to cause feelings of jealousy and envy. Always make sure you are cautious of the people you surround yourself with.
- **Some people will bring you toward your goals and dreams.**
  Ten percent of people will get into the trenches with you to help fight for your dream, as well as motivate you to achieve it. They may show in steps to get your dream; depends on if they did the same thing that you want to do. You definitely need to listen because it may bring you closer to what you want to achieve.

Thought Process
- Sometimes you have to shift your mindset.
- How do you shift your mindset?
- **Follow everything your mentor shows you or tells you. This is one way to shift your mindset.**
  If you have a mentor, this may be the key you need to nurture and develop your thought process. Your mentor will know what is needed and/or what it takes to recondition your entire thought process.
- **Read a positive book.**
  When you read a positive, motivational book, you could easily re-equip yourself with the tools needed to shift your thought process to achieve your goals and obtain endless possibilities.
- **Doing the mundane thing until your brain thinks it is second nature.**
  Always remember the little things add up. It will strengthen your mindset because that is what God has given you. It's the 1% things that over time will become so powerful that you will never be able to be taken off course to reach your dreams.

Think Clearly
- You always have to think clearly?
- How could you start to begin thinking clearly?
- **Find something to help you maintain focus.**
  If you have a mentor, he/she might have something called a mastermind. A mastermind is when a group of people come together with a common purpose and goal. Remember- you may have to breathe sometimes to turn stress into determination.
- **Talk to your mentor.**
  Your mentor can always assist you with your goals. He/she will be able to show you how to have a focused vision and think clearly. You will also need to self-reflect.
- **Always read your notes.**
  Sometimes it is a good thing to go over your notes as a refresher.

Your brain only comprehend 15% of what you hear.

Stop Stressing
- You have to learn how to breathe.
- What steps can you take?
- **Meditate.**
  Sometimes you will have to clear your mind in order to focus. Meditation is a great source to reduce stress and clear your mind.
  You can use these steps.
  How to meditate in 10 easy steps
  Step 1: Before you get started. Before you start, you need to take care of a few practicalities.
  Step 2: Get settled. Find a quiet space where you can relax.
  Step 3: Breathe deeply.
  Step 4: Check in.
  Step 5: Scan your body.
  Step 6: Consider the 'why'.
  Step 7: Observe the breath.
  Step 8: Allow your mind to be free.
  Step 9: Prepare to finish.
  Step 10: Take it with you.
- **Read a motivational book.**
  Reading a positive book can reduce stress, which will allow you to accomplish your goals. When you have less stress, you are ready to receive the blessings God has in store for you. Do not miss a blessing because you are stressing.
- **Do something that interests you.**
  You can always find something that you like, such as golf, chess, swimming, basketball, etc. When you begin to stress, choose a hobby or interests to invest in that you find enjoyable.

Observations
- Pay close attention.
- What are things you find yourself paying attention to?
- **Whatever your mentor is doing, do it also.**
  It's always good to mimic whatever your mentor is doing well; keep in mind he/she is doing what you want to do. If you want to make $5,000/per month and your mentor has accomplished that, pay close attention if your mentor is willing to show you how to reach our goals.
- **Do not pay attention to negative people.**
  At times, negative people will tempt and/or prevent you from following your vision. Do yourself a favor- do not listen to them. They will only bring you further away from achieving your dreams. These distractions may present itself as complaints and negativity. They will never come to you with positivity, unless they are a positive person.
- **Look at positive, successful people.**

Always pay close attention to how successful people live their lives- the way they walk, talk, and dress. You have to understand the reasoning and importance of certain words and actions. If they have reached their potential, you will see it in their body language. I encourage you to always be aware and observe what they are doing. If it is something you would like to do, follow their example.

What Is Your Mentality?

- Who is stopping you?
- How would you become aware of obstacles?
- **You are the only enemy that can stop yourself from achieving your goals.**
  When you start to allow self-doubt to enter your thoughts, something may happen that will negatively impact your mindset to reach your potential. You could be close to your blessing, but self-doubt and negative self-talk may prevent you from receiving it. It may pull you further away from your dreams that you want out of life. Just be careful of your self-talk; however, sometimes you may need to argue with yourself to gain shift your mentality. For example, you could look in the mirror and take a hard look at yourself. You can always be the reason you are not reaching your dreams.
- **Do not allow yourself to stop paying close attention to your dreams.**
  You are the only one who can lose focus on your dreams.
- **You begin to allow negative thoughts to enter into your mind.**
  You can be blinded by your own negative ideas. It could also stop you from achieving your vision. You have the choice to make a difference in the world. Like a wise man once said, "If the mind can conceive and believe then the mind can achieve." You will always be the master of your destiny. We can go a lot further together than we can alone. You have to know how to handle your blessings that God has for your destiny. You always have to believe in yourself- no matter the circumstance or your "why." The way I look at it- the biggest battle you will ever have to face is when you battle yourself. All you need to do is go with the flow and keep your faith up.

Negative vs. Positive

- You always have choices.
- What kind of choices will you make?
- **If you listen to 5 negative people, you will become number 6.**
  You always have to watch out because negative people do not have your best intentions at heart. You should always keep your distance because negativity impacts your ability to achieve your goals. They want you to stay where they are.
- **If you listen to 5 positive people, you will become number 6.**
  Try to surround yourself with people that are positive and successful, because they may have what you want or trying to accomplish. Stay close to them.
- **Watch out for who is trying to influence you.**
  Some people are there for you; however, some simply are not. You have to identify the difference and pay close attention. It is your own destiny. You have to make the choice- just remember the choice is always yours to make.

Open Your Mind
- Expand your spaces.
- What does expansion mean or look like?
- **If your desire is bigger than your want, then the possibilities are endless.**
  Always remember the bigger your desire will outweigh your want. You will always think about solutions to get what you desire.
- **You have to think thoughts.**
  Keep in your mind that you will achieve your dreams, so you will need to open your mind and think clearly.
- **The universe doesn't know what you want, but gives you what you speak.**
  Be careful of the words you speak. If you say something negative, the universe will give it to you. It is the same concepts as when someone says, "I'm having a bad day," or "I wish I wasn't late for work." They end up having a bad day or even being late for work. What if you shifted your mindset? What if instead of speaking negative thoughts, instead you speak positive thoughts, such as "I am going to have a good day." Also, whatever you envision, say it aloud to the universe. But the choice is yours- you choose!

Vivid Visions
- Expand different dreams.
- What picture could you think of?
- **You can get pictures of what your vision is.**
  Look at actual pictures that align with your vision. For example, the house you want in detail or the car you want to drive. Whatever you want- get the pictures. Look at the pictures every day.
- **You can create the vision around the house.**
  You can put your pictures of your vision on the walls around your house. Sometimes you may need to set up your vision within your environment as a constant reminder to reach your goals. This will allow you to have a mental image of your vision everywhere you go.
- **Write down your vision.**
  You can get a 3x5 index card, journals, post-it notes, and/or notebooks to write down your vision. You would want to write down what you want every day and continue to read it wherever you go. Looking at it before going to sleep each night and first thing every morning, as a constant reminder.

Light a Fire
- You have to find something that boils your blood.
- How are you supposed to do that?
- **Think about what drives you.**
  When you think about your vision and dreams, let that be a fire that burns your blood. You will feel the need to get done whatever needs to be in order to achieve your dreams. You will find motivation and will not allow anyone to stop you from getting to your finish line.
- **Whatever negative people say to you or about you, let that fuel your fire.**
  Negative people will always say bad things, such as "You will never be able to do that," or "They are just getting you for your money." Sometimes you may even hear, "You aren't making any money from that, so you just need to quit." So you can take

that criticism and used that as like fuel in your mind until you can prove them wrong. Let me paint a mental picture. Just like you put fuel in your car to get you to your destination. Your brain is the car and their criticism is the fuel.

- **Y**ou **can always get your fire started by watching and seeing what other positive people do or say to you.**

    Watch what people say to you because positive and successful people could spark something inside of you that will boil your blood. I encourage you to work with a positive mentor that has a successful mentality and work ethic.

Why is Your Why?

- What is your vision?
- What drives you?
- **Write down what you want to do in life. Find a way to achieve it. Keep your mindset focused on your vision. You have to have laser focus.**
- **Be specific on what you want.**

    Always have in detail what is you are envisioning for your life. Make a list of all the things you want and set goals to achieve each them.

- **Collect pictures of what you want.**

    The pictures are for you and different people to look at. When people say you won't make it or you will not reach your goals, just look at the pictures of your dreams because that is what you are fighting for. When people ask why you are doing what it is you are doing, they can see the pictures that represent your "why." Just remember, you don't just get what you want. You get what you speak and envision.

M is for Merry, abundant joy
I is for Immaculate, striving for perfection
N is for Noble, self-sacrificing
D is for Distinguished, most outstanding

O is for Orderly, ever organized
V is for Victorious, you're a winner
E is for Entertaining, a bundle of fun
R if for Radiant, you are a shining light

M is for Mature, you always know what to do
A is for Active, brimming with energy
T is for Thoughtful, considerate towards all
T is for Tender, a gentle soul
E is for Endearing, so loveable
R is for Reflective, How I can be more

Chapter 2
From Childhood to Adulthood

- *Tender Age*
- *Carefree*
- *Pressure from Parents & Bullies*
- *Teen Thoughts*
- *Clouded Minds*
- *Adulthood*
- *Loss of Dream*

Tender Age
- Be careful of what you do.
- Why do we need to be careful?
- **Sometimes parents do not think before they say or do something in front of their children.**
  You have to realize that children will do whatever their parents do or say, such as the common saying "Monkey see monkey do." Be mindful of your daily actions and patterns.
- **Children often look up to their parents and some parents take that for granted.**
  When children do something well and want their parents approval, sometimes their parents may not respond as desired. For example, if a parent is having a bad day, a parent may snap at a child vs. giving words of encouragement. Parents may not even realize their words have hurt the child. Unfortunately, this may cause children to act out as a response. Parents need to pay attention to their words and actions.
- **Parents and children need to be on the same page.**
  When their children do something well, parents need to acknowledge their child's achievements and give praise when needed. At least they can give the child a hug and give words of encouragement. Most children want to be acknowledged by their parents.

Carefree
- Children are so carefree.
- What does carefree mean or look like?
- **They are so open-minded.**
  Children are so happy and grateful for just the idea that anything is possible. Children feel like they can do anything as long as you put your mind to it.
- **Children can think ups some crazy things.**
  Children can have wild imaginations. They can come up with some ideas and think they can do or be anything in the world. If they think that they want to be a superhero, children can actually visualize themselves as a superhero. You may see a child imagining he/she is flying around the house. Do not tell a child to stop because then you will be stopping his/her imagination.
- **Parents need to sometimes "play along" with their children.**

If parents would actually play with their children or understand their child wants to be a superhero, children would be encouraged to use their imagination. Why don't parents want to be the "bad guy"? Parents can tell children if he/she wants to be a superhero, a hero could be a firefighter or police officer. Do not bash a child's dream, but join them.

Pressure from Parents & Bullies

- Recognize children may be under different amounts of pressure.
- What are some types of pressures a child may face?
- **Parents may be the source of pressure for children.**
  Children are pressured by not pleasing their parents. For example, a child may be hesitant to play with something around the house, such as a sheet or a chair, because of the fear of punishment. This prevents children from being able to use their imagination during play.
- **Parents may not even realize the pressure on their children.**
  When parents see children not following expectations, it is not always because they are being the bad guys. It is because the parents are not acknowledging their children. When their children are doing something well, parents may not be giving recognition. Parents need to know when to give positive praise and encouragement to their children. Children desire acknowledgement from their parents.
- **Children also have pressure from bullies.**
  Most parents do not even realize that children can be under immense amounts of pressure from bullies. A child may or may not be comfortable to communicate with parents these outside pressures. Children may face fear when attempting to communicate with parents due to the possibility of not being understood or heard. I have personal experience with this situation. I used to get bullied a lot in school from 1st- 3rd grades, until my mom put me into martial arts classes. She enrolled me in classes because she was tired of me coming home crying after school. I felt like I was hopeless, but after learning martial arts I was never bullied again.

All I'm saying is be careful how you treat your children because they are our future.

Teen's Thoughts

- Teenagers may encounter feelings of self-doubt within their lives.
- Why do teenagers doubt themselves?
- **Memories of their childhood may still linger within their minds.**
  When a child becomes a teenager, he/she may ask, "Why do my parents see me as a screw-up?" See parents do not understand that they are responsible for their actions, such as how they are treating their children. When a parent constantly yells, it puts the child down. Be careful the words you use with a child because your word will stick with them.
- **Teenagers will rebel against their parents.**
  Look at teenagers act now. Some talk back to parents or rebel against authority. They don't feel like you care for them because when they were a child they may have been put down or discouraged in different forms.
- **Teenagers won't tell their parents what is going on inside their minds.**

When teenagers have issues it funny how they will never talk to their parents about it or confide in someone. This is the reason why so many teenagers join gangs because they may find the love and support within a gang they may have been searching for. A gang or another group of people, may make a teenager feel accepted and appreciated. Parents need to realize how words can be hurtful and have a lasting impact.

Like for example, when I am downtown performing magic, children will approach me and you can see the excitement on their faces- asking for another trick. Then I find parents will yell at the child, "No! Get over here and let's go." This usually results in the parent becoming upset with the child and the child feeling defeated. Parents need to be aware of their actions because what if that child wanted to be a magician? But now their dream of becoming a magician is crushed. The problem when this happens is we are no longer allowing teenagers to have dreams, but to have wants.

Clouded Minds
- Teenagers may experience clouded judgement.
- How do their minds become clouded?
- **Sometimes teenagers might not know what they are wanting.**
  Teenagers use to have dreams in childhood but may lose focus as they grow up. This results in unfulfilled dreams and aspirations because they may have simply listed to the wrong person. Like me, I knew I was destined for greatness. However, I faced a lot of judgement and criticism. I have even been told that I would never amount to anything, but I chose not to listen until self-doubt creeped into my mind. Then I lost focus on my dreams as I grew-up.

  You are the parent that can change this toxic cycle.
- **Communities could potentially impact a teenager's mindset.**
  Be sure to always pay close attention to what is happening within your community. Individuals within a community can either positively or negatively impact the youth. I say we need to pay better attention to our children and youth, such as the music listened to. We need to encourage and support their dreams and ambitions. They are our future.
- **Parents may be a cause of clouded judgement.**
  Parents need to motivate and support their children's dreams and visions, even as they transition to adulthood because when reality hits them, their vision may become clouded and viewed as unattainable.

Adulthood
- Adult's minds are trapped inside reality.
- What do you mean trapped inside reality?
- **Adults' minds are programmed by the day-to-day experiences and realities.**
  As adults, our thought process is focused on working a traditional job, paying monthly bills/expenses, and maintaining our homes because these are all primary impactors on day-to-day experiences. The issue is adults have been taught to either

accept circumstances or complain without acting. You see the problem with not doing something differently you should not expect to experience anything different.

- **When adults are children, they have been taught what reality taught them.**
  When adults were children, we were taught to go to school, get good grades, and receive a diploma. Then we were taught to go to collection and get more good grades to graduate with a degree. Where 80% of college students will never find a job in their chosen field in which they have their degrees for. We were never taught to have or seek opportunity.
- **Opportunity scares adults.**
  Some adults fear potential opportunities because reality has taught to work, pay bills, and struggle. The truth of this reality is it impacts the decision to either reject or accept a new opportunity.

I look at it this way-if God gives an opportunity, how dare you not take it because he will take it from you and give it to someone else who will utilize it.

Loss of Dreams
- Adults always lose their dreams.
- How come they lose their drams?
- **Adult's dreams may be influenced by other individuals.**
  Some adults may have a dream, but tell that dream to the wrong person. Now, they have created an opportunity for someone else's doubt, opinions, and energy to negatively impact the vision. Not everyone will see the full potential of your dreams because your dream was not meant for others to understand.
- **Some adults are different from other adults.**
  There are some adults that will encourage you to achieve your dreams. Like for instance my mentor encourages me all the time. He gives his honest input and helps to identify steps to take to reach my full potential. Some adults are there to help, but the majority's purpose is to put you down. I encourage anyone to find someone to help you achieve your goals.
- **Where is the richest place in the world adults should know?**
  The cemetery is the richest place in the word because that is where people have died with multi-billion-dollar ideas that were never attempted or achieved because they allowed the negative influence and reactions of others to impact their life decisions. They lost focus on their dreams, so they died with their dreams intact.

Just think about what if one of your ancestors came up with the concept of the cellphone way back in the days before it was invented because someone told them "that's a stupid idea." Fast forward-now someone else invented the cellphone and profiting from it. Everybody talks on cellphones-we don't even necessarily use landline phones! What if your ancestor followed through with the dream? How would your life be different? Just think about that.

That's why I tell people to watch the words that leave your mouth. What if you talked to someone who told you about their dreams, but you we're too quick to shut down their ideas. All I am saying is be careful of what you speak because you might not be aware of the potential consequences.

Chapter 3
Face Your Fears

- *Oneirophobia*
- *Phronemophobia*
- *Gnosiophobia*
- *Decidophobia*
- *Cenophophobia*
- *Catagelophobia*
- *Agliophobia*
- *Demophobia*
- *Glossophobia*

Oneirophobia
- Fear of dreams.
- Why are people afraid of their dreams?
- **People are afraid to dream.**
  So many people bash other's dreams so badly, they will in return quit their own or may never want to dream again because they are afraid of what other people may say.
- **Sometimes when they want to dream again, they become scared.**
  People who lost their dreams normally have had negative people, including family members and friends, influence their actions. Then become bitter and angry because of the judgement received from others. In return, they may find themselves shutting down other's dreams.
- **Now 3 strategies you will need to get your dreams back.**
  - Stop listening to negative people.
  - Dust your dreams off the mental shelf.
  - Surround yourself with like-minded people who have dreams of their own.
  When the time comes, you will want to get achieve your dreams because you will want to be different from the 80%. It will benefit you in the end because I will tell you this-be different, dust your dreams off the shelf, and continue to reach for your goals. The rewards will be endless.

Phronemophobia
- Fear of thinking.
- Why are people afraid to think?
- **People are so afraid to think.**
  We were not raised to think, but to react first. This is completely backwards-we need to have the skill to think before giving a reaction, in order to better handle situations. Our actions come with two types of consequences-positive and negative. We need to first think of the type of consequence we are wanting and then choose our reactions accordingly.
- **Some people are afraid of what others may think of them.**
  Sometimes you may even find yourself asking "Will they even like me?" Sadly, this is the exact same question that replays in almost everyone else's mind. Your mind is a

terrible thing to waste. Sometimes you would want to think more about the possible opportunities you could receive. There are good rewards for you.

- **People will always think a specific way about you.**
  Certain people will always try to throw you off your game to make you mess up your thought process. Always make sure to reject negative thoughts and accept positive energy. You will need to keep a positive mindset, free of the fear of judgement from others. You have all the control when you think for yourself.
- **Now 4 strategies you will need to begin thinking for yourself.**
  - Read a motivational book.
  - Listen to your mentor.
  - Listen to motivational speakers.
  - Write down all of your ideas and continue to reference your list.

Gnosiophobia

- Fear of knowledge.
- Why are people afraid of knowledge?
- **Fear can stop you if you let it.**
  The fear of knowledge can hinder you. People are not used to thinking, they are used to knowing. If you find this is you, what should you do now? You will always want to gain more knowledge. You do not want to be the person in the room who talks much, but knows nothing.
- **Some people will always fight to be right, even when they are wrong.**
  Somethings do not matter to a person who thinks he/she knows it all. You can even get the accurate facts and he/she will continue to argue with you. I will tell you this- don't tell them but show them. Do not try to argue with them because you will most likely lose the fight. All you can do is just take a breath and let it go through one ear and out the other ear.
- **Here are 5 strategies you will need to seek knowledge vs. rejecting knowledge.**
  - Listen to your mentor; they may have more information or knowledge than you.
  - Listen to an inspirational speaker.
  - Find out who will help you get over your fear.
  - Think you can always improve your knowledge-base.
  Remember-just because you might know certain things doesn't mean you know everything. If somebody has more experience and knowledge, please listen to them.

Decidophobia

- Fear of making decisions.
- Why are people afraid of making decisions?
- **Some people were raised to make bad decisions.**
  We have control over the decisions we make. Now sometimes we may become confused when deciding and the confusion may impact future decisions. For instance, I did not like making decisions. I felt like I would always make a bad decision until began to work with a mentor and he has told me one thing that will forever change my thought process: OD on PD (overdose on personal development). This means eat, sleep, and breathe personal development. I have continued to listen

to this piece of advice and it has made me a better person. Do not be afraid to make decisions because every decision you take has the power to change your life.

- **Be careful with the decisions you make.**
  Somethings may cause you to make decisions based on the choices of others. I encourage you to pay attention to the choices you make. When making decision for others, it could potentially hurt you significantly. You need to make decision for the right reasons.
- **Here are 5 strategies you will need to make better decisions.**
  - Think clearly before making any decisions.
  - Listen to your mentor.
  - Talk to yourself in the mirror and listen to the words you are saying.
  - Write out your thoughts.
  - Record yourself talking through your decision.

  The process of making decisions is a natural, daily occurrence. Remember-think before reacting. The consequences from making positive, effective decisions are phenomenal.

Cenophophobia
- Fear of new ideas.
- Why are people afraid of new ideas?
- **People may shy away from a new or unfamiliar idea because they do not understand the vision at the time.**
  This fear causes individuals to remain stagnant. This causes individuals to reject new ideas, which results in no action being taken. They may lack the drive to follow or understand new ideas. Some individuals may even experience significant fear of new ideas, which they will even reject new ideas of other's. This fear may cause you to miss blessings from God.
- **Do not allow new ideas to scare you.**
  New ideas have the potential to bring blessings into your life, which could either positively impact yourself and the people around you. What if your new idea had the potential to impact the world? However, if fear is a present factor within your mindset, the word will never know the impact of your vision.
- **Here are 3 strategies you will need to conquer your fears.**
  - Listen to our mentor.
  - Have a mindset accepting of new ideas.
  - Stop limiting yourself because of the fear of judgment from others.

  You are in control of your own destiny. Do not let people destroy your ideas. Allow your ideas to shine brightly for the world to see.

Catagelophobia
- Fear of being ridiculed.
- What do people fear being ridiculed?
- **People will always be afraid of what other people may think of them.**
  Some people can be cruel, whether intentionally or unintentionally. Now if you can ignore the negative talk and judgment of others that is a skill that will take you far in

life. In life, you will experience haters, but you cannot let that bother you. The only reason someone may hate on your ideas is because of 3 key factors:

- Their own insecurities.
- They do not want to get let behind.
- They are simply jealous.

People may become jealous of your will to do what you have to do to change your lifestyle for the better.

- **When being ridiculed, do not respond with anger.**

  Anger has the power to hinder you from achieving your goals. When you begin to argue out of anger, only one person has the control and power within the exchange. Guess what? It isn't you.

  I used to always let people get under my skin. Then I would lash out, until my mother told me one thing that has always stuck with me. She said, "When writing your life story, do not let anybody else hold the pen." Always remember you are in control of your life. Do not let other people's judgments dictate the outcome of your life.

- **Here are 3 strategies you will need to overcome the fear of being ridiculed.**
  - Always consult with your mentor.
  - Listen to various personal development resources.
  - Write down everything positive in a journal to combat the negative judgments from others.

  These strategies will significantly help you to become bulletproof to the negative talk and judgment from others.

Agliophobia
- Fear of pain
- Why do people fear pain?
- **All we are designed to be afraid of pain.**

  A lot of people can handle pain. I am not talking about cuts and bruises. I am talking about the pains of life: physical, mental, and emotional. People are afraid of the pain of whatever life may throw at them. You can go through something so terrible that I will shut you down. A lot of people do not want to fight the pain. Instead, they decide to complain about it.

  Like me for instance, I used to buckle over the pains of life. I always struggled with certain events in my life, as you could see from my introduction, but I surrounded myself with the right people who helped me change that.

- **You will want to have a mentor who has gone through a similar struggle to help you deal with the pain.**

  You will always experience pain in your life. A mentor who has experienced similar struggles will be able to help you through your situation, such as the steps to take to overcome the pain. All you have to do is listen and do what he/she tells you.

- **Here are 3 strategies you will need to help you get over your fear of pain.**
  - Listen to your mentor.
  - Listen to personal development audios.
  - Listen to motivational speakers.

You need to believe in yourself. Once you believe in yourself you will be able to overcome anything you put your mind to. Never forget that. You will always have pain in your life, but what you do with the pain is your choice.

Demophobia
- Fear of crowds.
- Why are people afraid of clouds?
- **People are afraid of crowds.**

A person may be afraid to try anything new in front of his/her friends because of the fear of potential judgment. This feeling prevents someone for going for what they want in life. Instead, the choice is to remain with his/her broke-minded, negative friends.

I used to be afraid of what my friends may think. I used to keep my ideas locked up and just do whatever it was my friends were doing at the time. Sometimes we would sit around and talk about things of little importance-stupid stuff. Everyday we would do nothing to make our lives better. We would just go to work, hangout, and repeat. Every time I would try to do something that would change my life, they would just bring me down. I'm even talking about my own family, not just my friends. Finally, I became tired of struggling and having people bash my dreams who were not meant to understand it. Once I became tired, I changed my crowd.

Sometimes you have to get to the point where you are sick and tired of being sick and tired. Sometimes change may look like distancing yourself from friends and family members who are constantly putting your ideas down. You may need to change who you associate with in order to continue to reach for your dreams.

- **Sometimes it pays to change the crowd.**

If you find a set of new, positive people to hangout with, your life could potentially be different. People that have goals will are more likely to have your back and push you in the right directions to achieve them. They will not bash your dreams, goals, or ideas because they didn't let anyone bash theirs. They understand how to encourage you to achieve your dreams.

I was tired of struggling, so I made sure to position myself with the right group of people who could help elevate my mind and dreams. You should do the same because I do not want to see anyone else struggling like I have.

- **Here are 4 strategies you will need to get over your fear of crowds.**
  - Get a mentor.
  - Change your crowd from negative to positive.
  - Make a list of all the negative and positive factors within different crowds. Choose to be a part of the crowd that the positive outweighs the negative.
  - Listen to motivational speakers.

Just remember to decide between factors that will either positively or negatively impact your life. If you hangout with five broke-minded, negative individuals, then you will be the sixth broke-minded, negative individual. However, if you hangout with five positive, successful individuals, then you will be the sixth positive, successful individual. With these changes, you will be able to achieve anything you want in life.

Glossophobia
- Fear of speaking in public.
- Why do some people fear speaking in front of a group of people
- **The fear may be present since childhood.**
  When children are in school, sometimes they may be scared to talk in front of their classmates. They may fear the possibility of no one listening or even laughing at them. When children are young their minds are fragile. As they become older, they may still be afraid or shy to talk in front of crowds. Some people shutdown completely in front of a crowd. It is helpful if other people encourage them to speak in front of other people. Then when they become adults, the feeling of fear won't necessarily be there. Some people simply think they do not know how to speak in front of a crowd. Some people think that nobody will listen to what they have to say.

  Just like me, I always thought that people would make fun of me. I would never want to talk in front of a group of people, until I heard Les Brown. He forever changed my mind to speak in front of a crowd. If you don't know who Les Brown is, Google him. It is because of him that I wanted to become a motivational speaker.
- **Be careful of what you do.**
  You never know if you what you have been through could help somebody else in a similar situation. Let this notion inspire you to speak in front of people. You could be the voice that could save someone's life.

  I always say this, "You'll never know what a person has been through until you give a listening ear." You don't know what your decision of speaking in front of people can actually do in their lives. Just remember your destiny is determined by your next decision. Be careful of the decisions you make because it can set into motion a ripple effect for your life.
- **Here are 3 strategies you will need to conquer your fear of public speaking.**
  - Connect with a mentor and listen to the advice given.
  - Listen to motivational speakers.
  - Practice in front of a positive crowd or group.

  I will tell you this-always strive to help others. You could save someone's life with the knowledge you have because you never know what a person is going through.

FACE YOUR FEARS

F is for Fascinating, most engaging
A is for Artistic, full of creativity
C is for Creative, your works are most original
E is for Entertaining, a bundle of fun
Y is for Yearning, a thirst for experience
O is for Organized, you always have it together
U is for Uber, simple outstanding
R is for Regal, like a royal
F is for Forgiving, patient with others
E is for Effervescent, bubbling with life
A is for Accomplished, endowed with talent
R is for Rational, ever logical
S is for Sacred, a dear treasure

Chapter 4
Keep Strong

- *Be Bold*
- *Stay Alert*
- *Keep your Head Up*
- *3x5*

Be Bold
- You have to be bold in life.
- Why do you need to be bold?
- **People can sense when you are afraid or lack confidence in yourself.**
  When you think about something and you start to do it, be bold about whatever is it that you are doing. Never show any signs of weakness because people will see it. If you want someone to believe in what you are doing, you first have to believe in it yourself. How can you expect people to follow, if you cannot lead yourself? Remember to be bold and strong in everything you want in life.
- **Boldness is the most important thing to keep strong.**
  Sometimes it takes the right mindset to have the boldness you need to keep strong. When you have the right mindset, nothing will knock you off your game. The reason that people don't get what they want in life is because they lack the boldness to pursue it. They just want to talk about it, but never act on it.
- **The choice of being bold or not is up to you.**
  You have the power to be as bold as you possibly can. Now all you have to do is just to remember over and over again that you have the complete control on how bold you choose to be in life.

Stay Alert
- You always have to be on the lookout.
- Why do you need to be on the lookout?
- **There are some people whose role is to help you to reach your full potential.**
  Although there are people whose role is to help you, there is a majority that's role is to bring you down either directly or indirectly. You have to be able to identify which group you want to have in your corner.
  Family members may be the biggest influences to keep you from achieving your goals. Not all of your family will prevent you from moving forward, but you need to be able to recognize the difference and pay close attention to who is around you.
  Friends may also be a source of negativity. You may find some friends are incapable or simple choose not to support the positive direction you are heading, unless they are doing something positive too. You need to be able to weed out the bad ones. So many times people let the negative people influence them rather than positive people.
- **You need to pay attention to your environment.**

Your environment can make or break you, even prevent you from helping others. When you are around negativity, you will become negative yourself. Then you will have nobody who will want to be around you and will continue to attract negative people. In return, positive people will not want to be in your presence. Positive people love positive environments. They are at their best when they are surrounded by positivity.

Where do you want to be in life? No matter the goal, I will tell you people will envy you when you get your vision. Do not let their envy of you dictate the outcome of your life.

- **Be careful who you let in your environment.**

Always stay alert in regard to your environment. Be sure you are willing to accept the consequences of potential negativity or the blessings of positivity. I will never go back to that negative environment. My life has never been happier and more focused on achieving my dreams. You will always have to be on alert.

I want you to always choose to surround yourself with positivity, but I can't for your hand. All I can do is show you the difference between negativity and positivity. You will ultimately have to choose for yourself.

Keep your Head up
- You always have to keep your head up.
- Why it's important to keep you head held high?
  - **At times, life may bring you down.**

    When life brings you down, always think positively. You will always have problems in life; however, life is what you make of it. You have to focus on your end result, if it is a positive one. Then you will overcome any problems that you may come across.
  - **Life isn't the only thing that will bring you down.**

    People will bring you down with their negativity. They may also bring down your hope. Sometimes you have to ignore people that are negative and always keep your head up. I try my best to not allow any negativity within my environment and mindset. They do not breathe the same air as me. My whys are so strong that nobody can break me down. There are so many times when life and negative people attempted to bring me down, but I always keep my head up. You have to always remain positive and know that you will achieve anything you want in life. All you have to do is keep your head up.
  - **Here are 4 strategies you need to keep your head up.**
    - Listen to your mentor.
    - Listen to motivational speakers.
    - Read a motivational book.
    - Write positive moments and events in a journal. Reference the journal on a daily basis.

3x5
- Always keep 3x5 Index cards on you at all times.
- Why do you need to use index cards?
- **When you dream or have a vision, you will need 3x5 index cards.**

It is always best to write down your dreams and ideas. You always have to be prepared. A wise man once said, "It's better to be prepared for an opportunity than have an opportunity and not be prepared." I always like to be prepared because you never know when you might be able to get your vision on your index card. Once written down, someone could see you 3x5 card that is able to help you achieve the goals that are written. Always be prepared and read because you never know when it may be your time.

- **You might see or hear a positive quote somewhere that inspires you.**

    When you see or hear something that inspires you, write it down. If you write it down, then you will be able to reference back to it when you are needed some inspiration. Reference the card when you are feeling negativity or if someone is attempting to crush your dreams.

- **Always have 3x5 index cards on you.**

    I will tell you this. I look at my 3x5 index cards everyday. I not only read the cards, but I speak the words out loud into the universe.

Chapter 5
Passion

- *Emotion*
- *Devotion*
- *Intensity*
- *Fire*

Emotion
- You have to have strong emotions or your passion.
- Why do you need to have strong emotions?
- **What happens if you do not have strong emotions about your passion?**
    You will not have the right focus to get what you want out of life. Sometimes when you have strong emotions, your backbone will be so strong that you will let no one stop you from having a strong passion; no matter the want.
- **If you have strong emotions, it will help your devotion get stronger.**
    Let me tell you why emotions and devotion go hand-in-hand. You see in order to have strong devotions you have to have strong emotions. If you have strong emotions, then your passion will grow so strong you will achieve your dreams.
- **Always remember to keep your emotions strong.**
    If you have emotion behind your passion, then your mind will make it happen. Always keep your emotion and devotion strong to fuel the desire to reach your dreams.

Devotion
- You need to be devoted to yourself.
- Why do you need to be devoted to yourself?
- **Devotion is one of the 7 things you need to know about your passion.**
    The more devoted you are then the strong your passion will be. Sometimes people may say they're passionate about something, but their actions speak differently. You have to be devoted at all times. There are some things you need to be willing to sacrifice in order to devote more time to yourself. Remember whatever you are passionate about to devote yourself to it.
- **Sometimes by having a strong devotion in what you are passionate about, others may be watching.**
    People may always watch you because they want to see you fail. They are not interested in seeing you succeed in what you are passionate about. Now sometimes we have to be careful of what we do. Devotion of a passion is very important.
- **When you are devoted in your passion, you can accomplish anything.**
    You can achieve whatever you want to have for your future. Nobody will be able to deter you from your future or your vision. Like me, I will get what I want for my vision because I have strong devotion to my passion. My passion is to be an author and motivational speaker.

Intensity
- You will always have to intensify your passion.
- Why is this important?
- **The level of intensity will determine how much of your passion you have.**

    Now from time to time people lose their intensity. When this happens, loss of intensity allows the influence of other people to impact your ability to achieve your dreams. My passion is strong that my intensity level is a 10. I do not let anybody deter me from my goals. Remember to always fight for what you want.
- **Intensity is very important for another reason. *name the reason here**

    When people see how intense your level of passion is, they will be drawn to your vision because your passion is visible. When you speak about it, they may even hear the passion in your voice. Always be mindful of your intensity level because others may be watching.
- **Now when your intensity level is a 10, your passion will be unstoppable.**

    When your passion is strong, your vision becomes even bolder. Then you are more likely to achieve your dreams. When your intensity is strong, it doubles your passion. When your passion is strong makes your vision more clear.

Fire
- You will always have to light a fire under your passion.
- Why do you need to light a fire?
- **Amazing things happen when you light a fire under your passion.**

    You'll have a hunger drive about something that God gave to you and only you. It also starts from within yourself. You have to believe that nothing can stop you. You are the only one that can stop yourself. You are your biggest enemy and critic. Be strong and keep your drive because you can achieve anything you put your mind too.
- **Some people are not open to different things.**

    They lack the drive and ambition to have passion for what they love to do! Sometimes they are too quick to give up on their passions. If you can just hold onto your belief that you have the passion to get what you love, then your dream is worth fighting for.
- **What is your passion burning inside of you that the world needs to see?**

    Who's stopping you from moving forward? I think people need to get out of their own way and don't lose focus on your passion.

PASSION
P is for Popular, liked by all
A is for Affirmative, seeking the positive in others
S is for Smart, a keen intellect
S is for Sensible, you always do the right thing
I is for Influential, your opinions count
O is for Orderly, ever organized
N is for Noble, an honorable heart

Chapter 6
Determination

- *Craving*
- *Hunger*
- *Focus*
- *Meditation*

Craving

- You may have a craving for success that will increase your desire to achieve it.
- What do you mean?
- **People will drive for success when motivated by the success of others.**
    People will do everything in their power to fulfill that craving. They will become dedicated to finding a solution to get what they have been craving, even if other people will try to prevent them from their vision. You need to stay focused on your desire. If you can focus on your cravings, then you will ultimately get whatever you desire.
- **Some people will not care about what you are craving.**
    The only thing in someone else's mind may be "is that stupid or a scam" about what you are craving. It is weird because they only want you to stay where you are in life because they do not want you to pass them up or leave them behind.
- **Always stay focused on achieving your goals.**
    When you believe it, you will achieve it. You will receive your blessings from staying focused. Keep your craving for success strong and do not let anyone make you feel like you are incapable of success.

Hunger

- You need to have the hunger to fuel your desires.
- Why is hunger needed to fuel you desires?
- **You will always want to have hunger.**
    It will drive you to do things that seem impossible. Sometimes things may look like a wall trying to stop you from getting to your destination, but if you have the hunger to succeed then you will break through the wall. I used to let everything distract me until my mentor shared with my 2 things.
    - You have complete control over your thoughts.
    - Nobody can stop you accept for yourself.
        Never let anyone stop your hunger.
- **Do not lose your hunger based- off others.**
    People may lose their hunger and when that happens, may try their best to influence you to lose your hunger. You can feel the energy and vibes from them. *need further detail
- **Let your hunger for your desire be stronger than their hunger for failure.**
    Some people are comfortable where they are at in life because they do not possess the hunger to fuel their desire to win.

Focus
- Focus fuels your desire.
- How can focus fuel your desire?
- **Focus is the primary factor able to uplift your desire.**

    Some people do not have the strength to stay focused. What you need to do is find a way to build and develop your focus because if you can't focus on certain things then you need to consider changing that. You need to focus on the things you want and then have the desire to want to get it. Without focus, your desire will not grow, and you will lack the drive and energy to achieve your dreams.
- **It can be difficult to have focus.**

    I always had a hard time focusing on one thing, until my mentor helped me work on myself. When I had a goal, I used to always lose my focus. A significant part of that was of who I was associated with. I used to have negative people always talking in my ear negativity. It wasn't until I started to listen to my mentor and personal development on focus that I was able to change that. You must channel your mindset to learn how to focus by any means necessary.
- **Here are five strategies you will need to increase your ability to focus on your dreams.**
  - Learn personal development regarding how to focus.
  - Read positive quotes.
  - Read positive poems.
  - Write on a 3x5 ways to help you remain focused.
  - Record yourself giving self-advice and reflection on keeping focus.

Meditation
- Meditation allows you to clear your mind to help with your craving, hunger, and focus.
- What is meditation and how does it help?
- **Meditation is the foundation of your desire.**

    Without meditating, you will not be able to have a clear mind. This will result in losing focus on your hunger and cravings. Sometimes you can always have time to meditate. People may dislike meditation because they do not know enough information about it. Meditation is always beneficial when you are stressed, which stress is a primary factor in why people may lose their hunger and cravings. If you don't know how to meditate, you can always learn from someone else.
- **When you meditate, you must have knowledge about chakras.**

    Your chakra is key to your meditation. Some people have never heard of chakras or even realize that chakras are the center of spiritual power in the human body where psychic energy flows. Once you learn how to harness the energy to let it flow through your body, then you will be able to have a clear, calm mind. But even if one is blocked, you will not be able to achieve a clear mind. You may have negative thoughts and energy that is blocking your chakras. An illness may even block your chakras. Allowing energy to flow through all seven chakras will strengthen your desire.
- **Seven chakras of the human body. (Researched online)**

- Root chakra- represents our foundation and feeling of being grounded
  - Location- base of spine in the tailbone area
  - Emotional issues- survival issues (i.e., financial independence, money, food)
  - Color- red
  - Healing exercises:
    - Stomping your bare feet on the ground. Remember the root chakra is all about feeing "grounded."
    - Practicing Kundalini Yoga- able to open your lower spine
    - Bridge pose
  - Healing foods:
    - Red colored foods (i.e., apples and beets)
    - Hot spices (i.e., cayenne peppers and tabasco sauce)
    - Vegetables
    - Animal proteins (i.e., red meats and eggs)
- Sacral Chakra- represents our connection and ability to accept others and new experiences
  - Location- lower abdomen; two inches below the navel and two inches inward
  - Emotional issues- sense of abundance, well-being, pleasure, and sexuality
  - Color- orange
  - Healing exercises:
    - Pelvic thrust
    - Cobra yoga pose
  - Healing foods:
    - Orange colored foods (i.e., oranges and tangerines)
    - Nuts
- Solar Plexus Chakra- represents our ability to be confident and in control of our lives
  - Location- upper abdomen
  - Emotional issues- self-worth, self-confidence, and self-esteem
  - Color-yellow
  - Healing exercises:
    - Kundalini Yoga- boar pose
    - Dancing- shake those hips!
  - Healing foods:
    - Yellow colored foods
    - Grains and fiber (i.e., granola, whole-wheat bread)
    - Teas (i.e., peppermint and chamomile tea)
- Heart Chakra- represents our ability to love
  - Location- center of chest; just above your heart
  - Emotional issues- love, joy, and inner peace
  - Color- green
  - Healing exercises:
    - Bikram yoga

- Love, love, love! Simply opening our hearts to others is the best healing exercise
  - Healthy foods:
    - Green colored foods
    - Green tea
- Throat Chakra- represents our ability to communicate
  - Location- throat
  - Emotional issues- communication, self-expression, feelings, and truth
  - Color- blue
  - Healing exercises:
    - Shoulder stand
    - Singing and chanting
  - Healthy foods:
    - Juices and teas
    - All types of fruit
- Third Eye Chakra- represents our ability to focus on and see the bigger picture
  - Location- forehead between the eyes (i.e., also known as Brow Chakra)
  - Emotional issues- intuition, imagination, wisdom, and ability to make decisions
  - Color- indigo
  - Healing exercises:
    - Child's pose or other types of yoga poses with forward bends
    - Eye exercises
    - Herbal oil treatments
  - Healing foods:
    - Purple colored fruits
    - Chocolate
    - Lavender flavored spices or teas
- Crown Chakra- represents our ability to be fully connected spiritually; this is the highest chakra
  - Location- top of the head
  - Emotional issues- inner and outer beauty, our connection to spirituality, and pure bliss
  - Color-violet
  - Healthy exercises:
    - Meditation
    - Running and cardio activities
  - Healing foods:
    - Since the Crown Chakra represents our spiritual connection to our surroundings, this chakra does not benefit from healing foods. This chakra is more likely to benefit from clean and fresh air.

Now, that you have been given some basic information about chakras, here are a few additional resources.

- Read a book about chakras.
- Look at videos.
- Discuss someone knowledgeable with chakras.

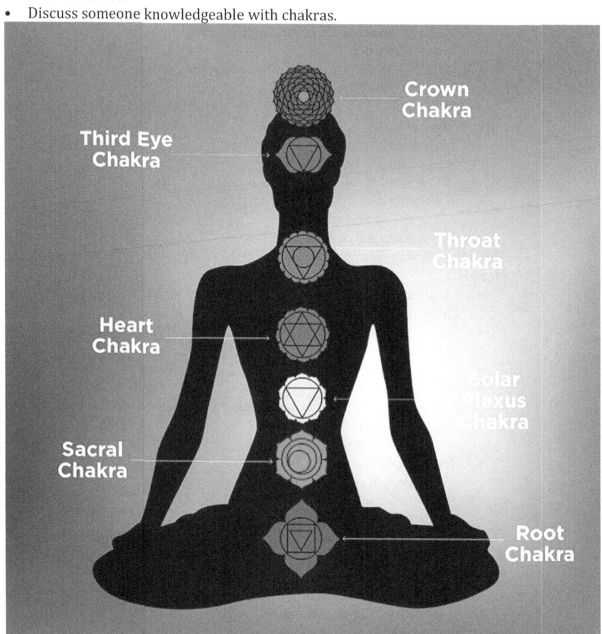

Picture from stylecaster.com

DESIRE
D is for Dedicated, Total Commitment
E is for Effervescent, Bubbling with Life
S is for Sensible, Always doing the right thing
I is for Impressive, An outstanding talent
R is for Radiant, You are a shining beacon of light
E is for Excellent, Of the finest character

Chapter 7
Determination

- *Courage*
- *Fearlessness*
- *Tenacity*

Courage
- You need courage to raise your determination.
- What do you mean?
- **Some people lack courage in all that they do.**

  You will have to make a decision. Either you are going to be afraid or you are going to get everything you desire. Courage is powerful; however, you will also have to see how courage can help you overcome any negative barriers.
- **Courage is the second main ingredient for determination.**

  There are some things that other people do not understand. When they do not understand your vision, they will criticize you because they do not understand the vision you have in your mind or your source of motivation. You will always have to have courage to continue to strive for your goals. Never loose focus on what you want to do. No matter what people may or may not say. Keep building your courage and it will make your determination stronger.
- **Here are 3 strategies you will need to help build courage.**
  - Always be positive and focus on what you believe in.
  - Surround yourself with people who will help you build your courage.
  - Self-assess as needed because your inner self may be your worst enemy.

Fearlessness
- You have to be fearless to fuel your determination.
- Why do you need to be fearless?
- **Fear can hinder you from achieving your dreams and stunt your determination.**

  When you are afraid, then anyone can say anything to you to influence you to give up on your dream. Some people love seeing other people afraid. It is like they feed on it. They can be negative against you and talk badly about you because they may even have fear themselves. You know what they say- misery loves company.
- **If you are fearless, then nothing or nobody will be able to stop you.**

  Sometimes you need to know what to do to become fearless. It could help you significantly and influence others to follow suite. Sometimes other people can benefit from seeing someone else handle situations fearlessly. To show them how you stand up to any fear you may have.
- **Here are 2 strategies you will need to become fearless.**
- Surround yourself with positive people that already have something going for themselves.

- Listen to motivational speakers.

Tenacity
- You have to have the right tenacity to fuel your determination.
- What do you mean?
- **You need to have tenacity to become stronger.**

     When people are able to see the strength of your purpose, you will be taken more seriously. Your purpose is your God given vision only that you can see and understand. Sometimes other people may lose their tenacity, while others may not even know what their purpose means. You can always tell if other people have tenacity. If you surround yourself with like-minded people, then your tenacity will grow stronger.
- **Like take my tenacity for instance.**

     I always wanted to make people laugh and smile. I always wanted to change the world. Despite my goals and dreams, I was told that I couldn't do it. I wanted to learn how to do impersonations, but I was always told that I wouldn't be able to achieve it. But guess what? My tenacity was strong.

Chapter 8
Who is in Your Inner Circle?

- *Pay attention*
- *Watch your back*
- *Control your surroundings*

Pay attention
- Always pay attention with whom you associated with.
- What do you mean pay attention?
- **People might not have the best intentions for you.**
  Analyze people to see if their intentions are genuine. You have to always be selective with who you allow in your inner circle. You have to be cautious. For example, if you want to be an author but your friend continues to put down your ideas then that is a negative influence.
- **So you want to stop being an author. Why is that?**
  Your friends may be afraid of being left behind because they do not want to change themselves. They will come to you with any and every negative influence. Pay attention and have discernment between positive and negative influences.
- **Here are 2 strategies you will need to pay better attention.**
  - Listen to how others talk with you. They will let you know if their intentions are genuine.
  - Seek out other positive individuals who have the same mind-set.

Watch your back
- You need to be cautious with who you allow to hang around you.
- What do you mean?
- **Need to know the intentions of people in your inner circle.**
  When you think you have someone behind you to support each step and find out they were just holding you back and that can be a very difficult and hurtful situation. You need to be able to find out who truly has your best interests at heart. Pick 5 people and assets in their lives. If your life is the same as theirs, ten your life isn't becoming better.
- **You have to change your surroundings.**
  If you are constantly surrounding yourself with friends who are broke and negative, you are most likely going to be broke and negative right along with them. So why not surround yourself with successful and positive people so that you can became successful and positive yourself.
- **You control your own destiny.**
  You can't always hang around the same people you grew up with because sometimes those same friends may not want you to change. Some of my friends didn't have my back when I began to make better decisions to improve my life. Instead of continuing to be negatively influenced, I found new friends that would support my dreams and help me reach my full potential.

Control your surroundings

- You always need to have control over your surroundings.
- Why do you have to have control of your surroundings?
- **You will allow yourself to be held back if you surround yourself with negative people.**

  You need to be very selective with who you let into your inner circle. Do not let anyone derail you from achieving your goals and dreams. You have a divine purpose in your life that once you find out what is it, you will have to have laser focus to achieve it.

- **Do not always listen to negative people.**

  Say for instance you want to become an author and your friend tells you that you are making a poor decision. You allow yourself to stop following your dreams because you listened to the negative influence. Why does that happen? I have always wondered the reasoning behind this. It is up to you to decide who and what you will choose to influence your decisions and mindset.

- **Sometimes change is needed with your inner circle.**

  My suggestion is to take a piece of paper and write 5 negative people and 5 positive people. Then choose who you want to be around.

Chapter 9
Overcoming Obstacles

- *Brick Walls*
- *Objection Hurtles*

Brick Walls
- You will come to a brick wall on your journey to attain your dream.
- What may brick walls look like?
- **Even when you have a clear picture of your dream, obstacles may appear in different forms.**

    You will have negative people trying to stop you from achieving what is meant to be yours. This is a brick wall that some people may never overcome. You can either let that stop you or motivate you to continue pushing forward. You need to develop a backbone and become bulletproof to the negativity. If you can break through the wall, then you will be able to accomplish anything.
- **Life can be a brick wall.**

    When people are on the verge of breaking through to their dreams, life hits them with an uppercut to the gut. When things become challenging it becomes easier for people to want to give up; however, you need to remain strong. Another barrier life may be is a financial barrier-not being able to afford the dream. For example, you may hear "I have bills, I have rent, I don't have this, and I don't have that." But then the next time you see that person, he/she is driving a brand new car or wearing a $200 pair of shoes.
- **Here are 4 strategies you will need to breakthrough a brick wall.**
    - You can find a great mentor.
    - Write goals on a 3x5 index card; refer to your goals daily.
    - Listen to personal development.
    - Read positive inspirational quotes.

Objection Hurdles
- People will face hurdles in their lives.
- What do you mean by that?
- **Hurdles can be a variety of things.**

    Hurdles can be: negative people, bills, rent, negative environment, yourself, self-doubt, fear, emotion, and lack of focus. Hurdles are the main reason why people experience failures in life. They can't see themselves jumping over the hurdles. When they see them, they may back down. We were not taught to overcome hurdles, instead we were taught to run from them. There are some people that are not afraid to overcome them. They are the 5% percent. You are the master of your destiny. Never give up and continue to fight to overcome hurdles.
- **I have had hurdles I have had to overcome.**

    I have had a lot of people try to stop me from achieving my dreams. I have faced many obstacles that I have had to conquer. With the help of my mentor, I was able to position myself to move forward. Now I do not let anyone stop me from reaching my potential. I have had life throw many things my way, but with the help of my mentor

I didn't give up. Sometimes you will always want to quit, it's only natural, but do not give into the feeling. Always be strong and never let anyone or anything become a hurdle keeping you from achieving your dreams.

- **Here are 4 strategies you will need to overcome hurdles.**
- Pick a mentor who can help you.
- Write down your goals and dreams on a 3x5 index card.
- Listen to personal development specifically regarding overcoming obstacles.
- Watch inspirational videos discussing how to overcome obstacles.

Chapter 10
Wisdom vs. Knowledge

- *Know the Difference*
- *Knowledge seeking*
- *Wisdom Imparting*

Know the Difference
- It is key to understand the difference between knowledge and wisdom.
- How can you tell the difference?
- **Here is the difference between wisdom and knowledge.**
    You can always see the difference between wisdom and knowledge just from the way people talk or converse with one another. If you repeat something that someone who was wise has said, then that is knowledge. If they say something that nobody has said then that is wisdom.
- **Here is how it will impact your life.**
    There is nothing wrong with the difference between the two because you need both to help you within your life. You will want to strive to have both knowledge and wisdom in your life because it may help you change someone's life. With wisdom and knowledge, you would position yourself to be able to teach other people or even thousands of people. Always remember wisdom and knowledge are both amazing things to have.
- **Here are 4 main characteristics to understand the differences between knowledge and wisdom.**
    Wisdom
    - It is something that God has given you like a thought.
    - Something that you have been thinking.
    - Something that you came up with.
    - Something that you can teach from your experiences.
    Knowledge
    - Something that has been taught to you.
    - Something that you learn from a teacher or other people.
    - Something you pick up from a book.
    - Something that you pick up from a mentor.
    Both are beneficial to your life, as well as needed to achieve your goals.

Knowledge seeking
- Listen and pay attention when someone with wisdom is speaking.
- Why is it important to listen and pay attention?
- **When someone with wisdom is speaking, you may want to listen.**
    You may never know what small little nugget you can learn. Now just think, can you know everything? The answer is no! Some people had to learn new things from one another. Do not ever let your pride prevent you from seeking knowledge.
- **You can always learn how to gain the knowledge you need.**
    What if a specific task comes up, but you do not possess the wisdom to achieve it? However, if you gain the knowledge needed you can change that. When things

seem easy to understand, always remember you learned wisdom from another person to help that task become easier. Always be prepared to learn and seek knowledge.

- **You need to be grateful to anyone who is willing to impart wisdom.**
  Never take for granted when someone is willing to share their knowledge with you. I am humble enough to listen because I am always open and willing to gain more knowledge. I encourage you to have these same traits because you may become the person with wisdom that is able to impart knowledge into someone's life.

Wisdom Imparting
- When you have gained wisdom, be open to sharing your knowledge with others.
- Why should we share our wisdom with others?
- **You should always want to pay it forward.**
  Never forget that you were once someone seeking wisdom. Now you will always have people seeking knowledge and other people may even waste your time. You need to be able to identify who you can truly help and move forward because time is the only factor you will never get back. Always utilize your time to be the most effective and productive.
- **You will be blessed when you share your wisdom and gifts.**
  Good things come to people who do great things. This is called the Law of Attraction. When you do something that is positive, such as giving people wisdom, you will have so many doors opened up for you.
- **Here are 3 strategies you will need to impart wisdom to someone.**
  - Need to find out the following factors: source of motivation, wants/needs, mindset, action plan to achieve goals, and goals.
  - Determine if that individual is willing and ready to work with you.
  - Make sure to have active listening and control the conversation.
  You are the one with the wisdom that they are seeking.

Chapter 11
The Life Map

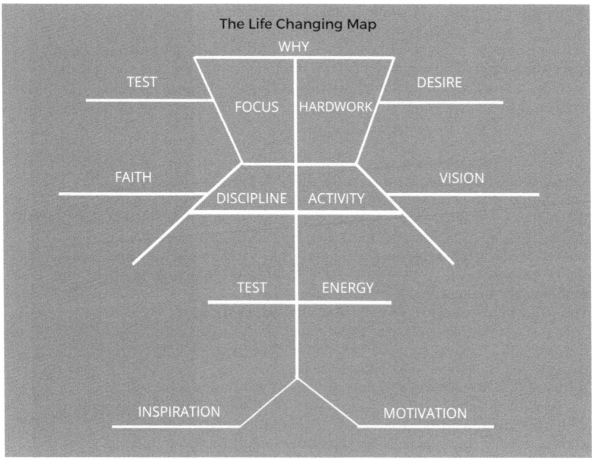

Designed at canva.com

What is a WHY?

The *why* is reason that drives you to accomplish whatever you set out to do. The *why* is your dream that you want in the future for your life. It is something that keeps you up at night. You may even want it so bad that you must get your emotions behind it. If you have your emotions behind your *why* then no one can stop you from getting your dream. Let me give you my *why* with 4 examples.

- I want to leave a legacy for my children. I want to leave a legacy, not just for all of them collectively, but leave a legacy for each individual child.
- I want to become a motivational speaker and author.
- I want to be able to help thousands of people because when I die and leave this earth I want to be remembered. I want to be remembered as someone who used their gifts to change the world, like Malcom X and Martin Luther King Jr.
- Now the one that we can all relate to and I'll just say it in one word- bills!

    You see these are some strong reasons. You must be able to see what is not there because only the ones who can see the invisible are able to do the impossible. You need to focus and work hard to achieve your *why*. I will breakdown how focus and hard work are the catalyst that fuels your *why*. There are 4 factors in each quality I want to outline for you.

Focus:
- Test- You must focus on what you want in life. You will always be tested with obstacles; however, if you can focus on the result then you will be able to pass any test life throws your way. Then you will be able to share your testimony.
- Faith- You must focus on your relationship with God. You need to know that God will not give you more than you can handle. Focus on the fact that God always has your back. Then you will be able to overcome any challenges.
- Time- You need to focus on the time you have and do not waste it. Time is the one thing you can't get back. Sometimes you need to take it one day at a time. Also, you must focus on the time you want to have to complete a goal that you have set. Do not focus on the time you have lost but focus on the time you have.
- Inspiration- You must focus on who or what you let inspire you, as well as who you are inspiring. Do you want to have negative people inspiring you? Or do you want positive people inspiring you? Always pay attention to who you are listening to because people may not always have your best interest in mind. Also, pay attention to who is watching you and who you are watching. If you associate with broke-minded, negative friends and family, you will find yourself broke-minded and negative. If you associate with successful, positive people then you will find yourself successful and positive. Inspiration is the key ingredient to your focus. If you have inspiration, you can overcome any test. Your faith will be stronger. You will not let anyone waste your time. Inspiration will also tie you with his twin, motivation, who we discuss shortly when we cover hard work.

Hard work:
- Desire- All successes start with your desire. Your desire is the fuel that drives your vision. If you have the desire to accomplish something, you must be determined to fight for it. It's either you want it or you don't. You can't have it both ways. It takes hard work.
- Vision- Everything comes from a thought. Your thoughts become things. Now your vision came from a thought. You must have a vision to get what you want in life. You don't get what you want-you get what you picture. When you have a vision, it takes hard work to get it accomplished.
- Energy- Hard work takes a lot of energy. What do you want to exert your energy on? Do not always rush into things because that may take a lot of energy and focus. You always want to spend your energy on doing something positive that will benefit you.
- Motivation- This quality is internal. It is a feeling you get from hard work and dedication. You must have the drive and resolve through motivation. You will always need motivation to push forward to reaching your goals. Here are a couple of examples on how to boost your motivation.
  - Listen to motivational speakers.
  - Read motivational books.

- Look at motivational quotes.
- Look at motivational poems.

These are just a few ideas to get you started. Remember dedication and motivation go together. You can get motivation from its' twin, inspiration, too.

These are the key factors to understanding focus and hard work. There are 2 other factors needed to bring together focus and hard work. Without these 2 factors, focus and hard work would not be possible.

- Discipline- This quality is needed in order to have focus and hard work to reach your *why*. Without discipline, you will have the choice not to achieve your dreams. Discipline is the primary factor that ties your focus and hard work together. They are the balance for you *why*. Just like Ying and Yang, without discipline focus and hard work cannot coexist with each other.
- Activity-You need activity to fuel your discipline. You must do the right activity to have discipline to have focus and hard work. You must have discipline to do the activity to get your *why* completed. Discipline and activity are the two factors needed to achieve your *why*.

Chapter 12
The Inner Map

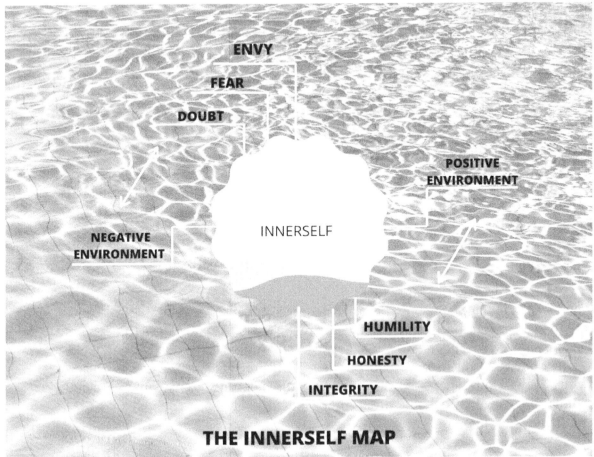

THE INNERSELF MAP

Designed at canva.com

The inner self is the hardest thing to recondition. It takes a lot of work change. Most people won't even try to change themselves, but they want something better for their life. Guess what? They will never get it. There are 2 things that will be the hardest battle you will ever face. The battle between a negative and positive environment. These two factors will determine how you overcome the battle between you and your inner self. Now I will go more in-depth about these contributing factors.

The Negative Environment

Now, in the negative environment your inner self will face three adversaries: doubt, fear, and envy.

Deprived	False	Enraged
Objectionable	Emotion	Negative
Unhappy	As	Vindictive
Belligerent	Reality	Yell
Terrifying		

You will always face challenges in these three areas. You must always be alert because you will have to identify who is in your life. Unfortunately, that may be one of the areas or all of them. Some people will have doubt in you because they know you from past experiences. Some people will try to make you afraid to go after what you want in life. Some people may envy you because they are begin left behind and upset with themselves. With these three adversaries, you will constantly battle with them internally. It is essential to not lose focus.

The Positive Environment

In the positive environment your inner self will face three qualities: integrity, honesty, and humility.

Imaginative	Honorable	Humble
Nurturing	Open	Upright
Terrific	Now	Miracles
Ecstatic	Esteemed	Instant
Great	Superb	Learn
Right	Trusting	Imagine
Idea	Yes	Thriving
Transformation		Yes
Yes		

This is the good side you want to be on. There are people who will show you integrity and you will know they have your back. They also would inspire you to achieve greatness. Some people will also be honest to you and do not sugar-coat anything. This group of people will want you to win. They also will show you how to have humility, which is the key to success.

You will always want to pay attention to these people because they want to see you win in life. Sometimes they may even mentor you to achieve your goals. You will have to choose the path you want in battle.

I Am
A Poem By
Ke Juan L. Moore Sr.

I am Ke Juan Moore Sr.

I am a Motivational Speaker
I wonder what it would feel like to change millions of lives
I hear the sounds of the crowd cheering my name
I see a stadium full of people
I want to win their respect
I am a Motivational Speaker

I pretend to focus on the time
I feel proud
I touch the stage and then I'm in my zone
I worry that people might now take me seriously
I cry when I think about trying not to fail in front of my kids
I am a Motivational Speaker

I understand how important my dreams are
I say always live by the 3 D's which is - your DESTINY is DETERMINED by your next
DECISION
I dream about speaking in front of thousands of people
I try to get better every day by working on my craft
I know my dreams will come true
I am a Motivational Speaker

Sometime you have to write a poem about what you want your future to be. A read it every
day so your sub-conscious mind can turn it into a reality.

YOUR

IS

BY YOUR NEXT

Designed at canva.com

Ninety percent of people:
- Are negative about opportunities because in school they were taught to have a job mentality. We are taught to go to school, get good grades, graduate with a diploma, and go to college. Once in college, we were taught the same cycle. However, These same individuals were not taught to have or get an opportunity.
- Always want stuff, but never try to do something to achieve it. So they do get what they want so they complain about it, until somebody has what they want and that person try to show or help them get it then they want to tell them no. You will never get anything you want in life as long as you keep on wanting and do not accept the help.
- Fighting over 10% of the money, such as jobs, food stamps, and ADC/Social Security Income. Therefore, people are struggling in life.

Ten percent of people:
- Believe they can do anything they put their minds to. They always define what they want out of life. Then they learn from someone who has accomplished similar goals because they understand that individual gets what he/she has pictured.
- Have a go-getter's mentality. They won't let anyone stop them from reaching their dreams.
- Split 90% of the money. They always have their money work for them. Specifically, five percent out of the 10% do MLM or Network Marketing because they believe in home-based businesses. Some become mentors to others. They know that if you are looking for a change then a change is looking for you.

You have to choose which side you want to be on, the choice is yours.

Chapter 14
The 9 Life Principles

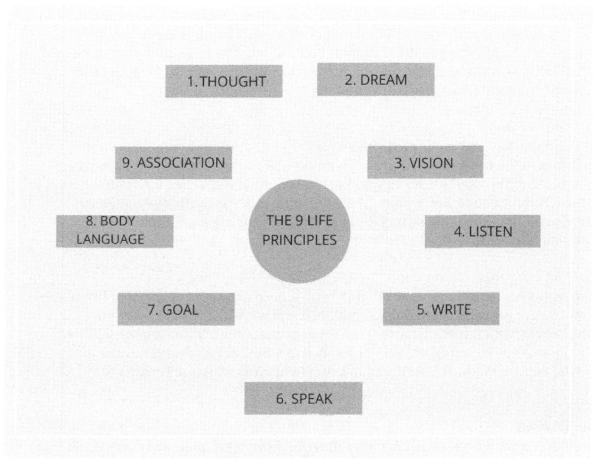

Designed at canva.com

Power of Your Thoughts

Thoughts are very powerful. You must protect your thoughts, whether your conscious mind and subconscious mind are working together or separately. Together they are processing thoughts that you want to have. Separately they are working in different ways. Here is how:

- Conscious mind- processes things that you can see
- Subconscious mind- processes things that you cannot see

Be careful what you are thinking because your thoughts become things.

Power of Your Dreams

Dreams are the end results of what you want in your life. Sometimes you want something so badly that you will dream about it. Your dreams will make your conscious mind think about it and your subconscious mind will make it happen. When you are dreaming, be careful of what you dream about. You will want to remember your dreams and write them down. Your dreams will manifest your outcome for you. Make sure to focus on what you want and never stop dreaming.

Power of Your Vision

Visions are the key ingredients to achieve your dreams. Visions are fuel for your dreams. It says in the Good Book – a person with no vision will perish. Sometimes you need to have strong visions to achieve whatever you want in life. Vision is the movie in your mind's DVD for you to watch your dreams manifest to reality. Always remember to have any visions and keep them strong for you to reach your dream. The end results will always manifest into reality.

Power of Just Listening

Listening is very important because some people need certain people just to listen. People are always going through tough situation. If you were just to lend a listening ear, your victory overcoming your obstacles could change someone's life. Listening will also show people that you care. You should not solely listen but should always be able to identify who you are talking to. You need to listen to identify who is negative and positive.

Power of Writing

Writing is essential because people need to write down their goals and dreams. This is a key step in reaching your vision for your life. You must have your visions written down and verbally state your visions out loud. When you write down your visions and say them out loud, you have claimed it in the universe. Now when you claim it, the universe will conspire to make it happen.

Power of Speaking

Speaking to the right person can change your life, as well as that person's life. People often don't speak enough, and some people speak too much. You have to know when and when not to speak. Speaking can help you to identify negative vs. positive people in your life. Be careful of the words you speak because there are consequences to what you speak.

Power of Your Goals

Goals are the marking points for you to achieve your dreams. A dream can be good, but your dream is dependent upon the goals that you set. By setting goals, you are giving the universe permission to give you your dreams. Too many times people do not set goals and that impacts their ability to reach their dreams. Always set goals because the choice is yours.

Power of Body Language

Body language can show you how someone is feeling. You should always attempt to read people's body language because body language is communication. If there is a millionaire talking to you, what would their body language say? You might want to mimic their body language, how they move, and how they walk. You always need to watch the body language of others because it will help you determine if that is a person you should be mimicking.

Power of Association

Association is everything. There are two types of associations: negative and positive. Negative association can influence you not to achieve your dreams. Positive association can help you to reach your true potential. It could also stimulate your mind to do anything you put your mind to. The choice is yours, so choose wisely.

COMFORT ZONE MAP

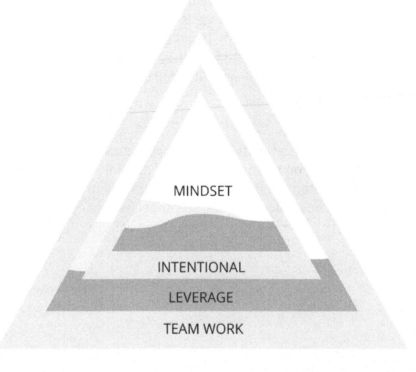

Designed at canva.com

Mindset- It's the right condition of the mind that you will be able to understand and process your thoughts.

Intentional- What you do on purpose to recondition yourself to have the right mindset.

Leverage- To lean on someone who has done what you are trying to do and willing to help you. Do not let your pride stop you from achieving the highest leverage needed to help you have the right mindset.

Teamwork- You must have the right mindset to be a part of a team of greatness because if you aren't in the best mindset then you are a cancer to that team. If you and the team are in the right mindset, then you will be unstoppable.

If you have the right mindset, being intentional, dependent on the right leverage, and right teamwork, then you will be pushed out of your comfort zone. Most people do not like to be outside of their comfort one; however, that is the reason why people do not achieve their dreams.

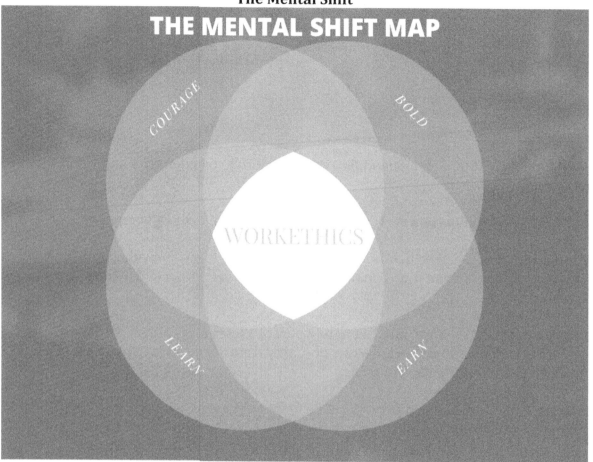

Designed at canva.com

Work ethics- It is when you produce hard work that you will be able to receive blessings coming your way.

Courage- If you have courage to have the right work ethics, then you can do anything you put your mind to.

Bold- You must be bold about having the right work ethics because it will be difficult.

Learn- You need to be willing to learn. You need to be teachable and coachable to learn how to be able to have a better work ethic.

Earn- You must be willing to accept whatever it is that you will earn. No matter how small or big it might be. You see the more you learn the more you'll earn.

Chapter 17:
Understand Your Personality Colors

- *Blue*
- *Green*
- *White*
- *Red*
- *Yellow*

Blue: Motivated by Intimacy
- Individuals are driven by intimacy and connecting and creating quality relationships. They bring great gifts of quality and service. These individuals are generally loyal, sincere, and thoughtful.
- Strengths:
    - Caring
    - Dependable
    - Loyal
    - Analytical
- Limitations:
    - Worry
    - Judgmental
    - Hard to please
    - Perfectionist

Green: Motivated by Money & Security
- Individuals are driven by money, security. They may desperately want to feel secure in both their finances and relationships. They are the domineering type and strive for brilliance, proficiency, and expert in all things.
- Decisiveness- strong at making timely decisions
- Expressiveness- encourage them to speak up rather than avoid issues
- Enthusiasm- calm personalities are sometimes misinterpreted as lacking interest
- Confidence- difficult time with giving themselves credit for actions

White: Motivated by Fun
- Individuals are driven by staying calm and balance. They may be peacekeepers. These individuals may bring great gifts of clarity and tolerance. They are generally kind, adaptable, and good listeners.

- Strengths:
  - Kind
  - Patient
  - Accepting
  - Devoid of ego
- Limitations:
  - Lack communication to share emotions
  - Express conflicts
  - Unwilling to set goals
  - Dislike working at someone else's pace
  - Self-depreciating

Red-Motivated by Power
- Individuals driven by power. They are typically strong leaders and actions are considered oriented and proactive.
- Strengths:
  - Assertive
  - Action-oriented
  - Determined
  - Focused
  - Confident
- Limitations:
  - Selfish
  - Arrogant
  - Need to always be right
  - Bossy
  - Aggressive
  - Demanding

Yellow-Motivated by Fun

- Individuals driven by fun. They are the fun lovers and enjoy living life in the moment. This group may bring great gifts of enthusiasm and optimism. They are generally charismatic, spontaneous, and sociable.
- Strengths:
    - Fun-loving
    - Carefree
    - Insightful
    - Trusting
    - Spontaneous
    - Sociable
- Limitations:
    - Uncommitted
    - Self-centered
    - Impulsive
    - Vain
    - Afraid to face facts
    - Unfocused

(researched online)

Now in 2020 I am a motivational speaker and I own my own company in which I am help other people change their lives and I just want to say it was thru the grace of GOD that I'm in the position to live a better life always remember the 3 D's that I live by every day.

*Your **DESTINY** is **DETERMINED** by your next **DECISION** !*

Made in the USA
Middletown, DE
05 November 2022

13998296R00038